A-9-09   X

EDGE BOOKS

Prepare to Survive

How to Survive a

FLOOD

by Matt Doeden

Consultant: Al Siebert, PhD
Author of *The Survivor Personality*

Capstone
press®
Mankato, Minnesota

Edge Books are published by Capstone Press,
151 Good Counsel Drive, P.O. Box 669, Mankato, Minnesota 56002.
www.capstonepress.com

Library of Congress Cataloging-in-Publication Data
Doeden, Matt.
    How to survive a flood / by Matt Doeden.
    p. cm. — (Edge books. Prepare to survive)
    Includes bibliographical references and index.
    Summary: "Briefly presents specific survival strategies that can be used in a
flood" — Provided by publisher.
    ISBN-13: 978-1-4296-2277-6 (hardcover)
    ISBN-10: 1-4296-2277-6 (hardcover)
    1. Floods — Juvenile literature. 2. Flood control — Juvenile literature.
3. Survival skills — Juvenile literature. I. Title.
GB1399.D64 2009
613.6'9 — dc22   2008030622

Editorial Credits

Carrie A. Braulick, editor; Veronica Bianchini, designer; Wanda Winch,
    photo researcher; Sarah L. Schuette, photo stylist; Marcy Morin,
    photo shoot scheduler

Photo Credits

Alamy/Bob Pardue, 12; AP Images/CP, Deddeda Stemler, 10; AP Images/David J.
Phillip, 17; AP Images/Fort Collins Coloradoan/Sherri Barber, 8; AP Images/Gemunu
Amarasinghe, 26; AP Images/The Herald-Mail/Kevin G. Gilbert, 18; AP Images/
Steve Helber, 4–5; Capstone Press/Karon Dubke, 13, 14 (all), 29; FEMA News Photo/
Andrea Booher, 28; FEMA News Photo/Jocelyn Augustino, 15; Getty Images Inc./
AFP/AFP, 27; Getty Images Inc./AFP/Byun Yeong-Wook, 9; Getty Images Inc./
AFP/John Russell, 7 (bottom); Getty Images Inc./China Photos, 22; Getty Images
Inc./Discovery Channel Images/Jeff Foott, 24 (bottom left); Getty Images Inc./
Minden Pictures/Michael & Patricia Fogden, 24 (bottom right); Getty Images Inc./
National Geographic/Annie Griffiths Belt, 7 (top); iStockphoto/Karen Merryweather,
cover; Landov LLC/Reuters/BEAWIHARTA, 11; Library of Congress, Prints &
Photographs Division [LC-USZ62-60479], 16; Peter Arnold/James Gerholdt, 24
(top left); Peter Arnold/Matt Meadows, 24 (top right); Rod Whigham, 19, 21, 23,
25; Shutterstock/Cheryl A. Meyer, 20; Shutterstock/Lora Liu, backcover (grunge
notebook); USDA/NRCS/Lynn Betts, 6

Table of Contents

Chapter 1

CAUGHT IN A FLOOD!

A flash flood can turn a peaceful camping trip into a fight for your life.

You're on a camping trip with your family. It's been raining for two days. You're walking back to your camper from the campground's activity center. Suddenly, cold, murky water rushes toward you. It's a flash flood! The water is around your ankles, climbing toward your knees. The strong current is almost pulling you down.

What should you do? Should you stay put, struggling to stay upright? Or should you turn around and run as fast as you can to the nearest hill? Do you have what it takes to survive one of nature's deadliest disasters?

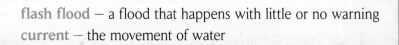

flash flood — a flood that happens with little or no warning
current — the movement of water

Floods fit into different categories. Some floods rise slowly over time. These floods often occur when rainfall or melting snow overflows riverbanks. Flash floods can happen almost instantly. For example, heavy rainfall could cause streets to flood suddenly. It could also cause a dam to break, sending millions of gallons of water down a river. Hurricanes can blow a huge storm surge onto shore. Tsunamis can roar onto an ocean coastline and travel miles inland. All of these floods are life-threatening.

Floods are one of the most common natural disasters in the United States. They are most common near waterways, but floods can happen anywhere — even in deserts. Flood victims have to think fast to stay alive.

storm surge — a large wave that is pushed onto shore
by the high winds of a hurricane
tsunami — a large, destructive ocean wave created
by an underwater earthquake

A hurricane's strong winds can reach 150 miles (241 kilometers) per hour.

Monstrous tsunamis can roar onto the coast and catch people off guard.

7

FLOOD DANGERS

Floods are dangerous for many reasons. The most obvious danger is drowning. Floodwaters can have strong currents. Even the strongest swimmer may not be able to swim against the currents.

Floods often come with severe weather. High winds can knock down power lines. Water conducts electricity easily. If you get too close to a downed power line, you could get an electrical shock.

TIP: Never walk through moving floodwater. Just 6 inches (15 centimeters) of rushing water can knock you off your feet.

A NASTY MESS

Floods can also make a nasty mess. Floodwater may stick around for days or weeks. Sewers and sanitation systems may back up or overflow. That means bacteria and toxic chemicals can leak into the floodwater. And that's not all — dead animals and even dead people could be floating in floodwater. All of these things make floodwater breeding grounds for disease. Just touching the water can be dangerous. Drinking it can be deadly.

bacteria — one-celled, microscopic living things that exist all around
you and inside you; some bacteria cause disease.
toxic — poisonous

Flood victims may wait in line for hours to get safe drinking water.

NOT A DROP TO DRINK

After a flood, you might be surrounded by water but not be able to drink it. Bacteria from floodwater can get into city tap water and private wells. Days or weeks could pass before tap water is safe to drink again. A healthy person can survive only about four days without water.

TIP: If you must drink tap water before local officials say it is safe, boil it for five minutes first. Boiling the water will kill most bacteria.

Chapter 2

HOW TO SURVIVE

TIP: Keep an emergency gas shut-off wrench in your home. This tool fits most household gas valves.

Would you know what to do if the water started to rise? No survival method is fail-proof. But knowing some survival tips will increase your chances of surviving a flood.

IF YOU HAVE PLENTY OF TIME

If you're lucky, meteorologists will issue a flood watch or warning for your area days before a flood occurs. A flood watch means flooding is possible. A flood warning means that flooding is occurring or that it will occur soon. With this notice, you can try to protect your home before the flood arrives. Walls of stacked sandbags can stop floodwater from coming into your house. Often, entire neighborhoods work together to fill and lay sandbags.

Watches and warnings also give you time to evacuate the area before a flood strikes. You may be tempted to stay home to protect your property. But your home can be rebuilt — you can't!

Before evacuating, turn off the natural gas in your house. Leaking gas after a flood could cause an explosion. Also disconnect electrical appliances.

A one-quarter turn of the gas valve shuts off the natural gas supply.

meteorologist — a person who studies and predicts the weather
evacuate — to leave an area during a time of danger

13

IF YOU HAVE LITTLE WARNING

Sometimes you'll get a warning less than a day before a flood strikes. But you can still prepare. Stocking up on food and bottled water is the most important thing to do. Buy lots of canned food that doesn't need to be cooked. If your area gets lots of floods, always have extra bottled water and canned food on hand.

What if you don't get enough warning to get to the store? Clean your bathtub or sinks. Then fill the tub or sinks with clean water. You'll be glad you did if it's the only clean drinking water you have after a flood.

QUICK THINKING!

New Orleans, Louisiana, resident J. Michael Brown prepared for Hurricane Katrina in late August 2005. He sent his wife and children to Ohio where they would be safe. He bought extra food and bottled water. Then he and his wife's parents waited.

Brown's worst fears came true. The hurricane caused the city to flood. Brown and his relatives went to the upper floor before the water rushed into the house. Within minutes, 6 feet (1.8 meters) of water flooded the home. The water continued to rise, reaching a depth of more than 12 feet (3.7 meters).

Brown and his family stayed in the house for three days, waiting for help. Then Brown saw that the lower level of the house was filled with deadly cottonmouth snakes. Food and water supplies were running out. Brown knew they had to leave. They rode to safety on a boat owned by Brown's neighbor.

Brown's preparations helped keep him and his family alive. More than 1,000 other flood victims of Hurricane Katrina lost their lives.

Flooding from Hurricane Katrina

TO THE ROOF!

The people of Johnstown, Pennsylvania, thought they were prepared for flooding on May 31, 1889. Many people went to the upper levels of their homes. There, they waited for the water to stop rising. They didn't know that the worst was yet to come.

Rainstorms caused a dam near the town to burst. A wall of water washed down the river and smashed into the town.

Sixteen-year-old Victor Heiser was in his family's barn that day. His father signaled from the house to get to the barn's roof. Heiser hurried to the roof, where he watched the water slam into his family's home. The water was two stories high. Even the barn's roof wasn't high enough. The floodwaters swept Heiser away. Somehow, he managed to climb onto the roof of a tall brick house. Along with 19 other victims, he waited. The house stood, and Heiser and the others survived. The flood killed more than 2,000 people, including Heiser's parents.

Johnstown flood damage

What If

YOU'RE CAUGHT OFF GUARD?

Planning is important. But sometimes, there's little or no warning that a flood is coming.

If you find yourself in this situation, look for higher ground. Gravity carries water to the lowest level possible. The higher you are, the safer you'll be. You can climb to the roof of a sturdy building. Or run to the top of a hill. You can even climb a tree if there's no other place to go. The goal is simple — get out of the way of the water!

YOU'RE IN A CAR WHEN A FLOOD STRIKES?

Should you speed through the floodwater? No! Just 2 feet (.6 meter) of rushing water can wash your vehicle off the road. A car that is swept away could flip. The inside of a flipped car is one of the most dangerous places you can be in a flood.

Always drive your car away from floodwater. If that's not possible, stop your car. Open a door or a side window to get out of the vehicle. Then head to higher ground.

If your car is swept into deep floodwater, you'll need a different plan. First, try to escape through a side window. If you can't get the window down, press on the edge of it with a key or another pointed object. You can also try kicking it out.

If your car sinks before you can get out the window, wait until the car fills with more water. After the water has reached the level of your shoulder, open a door or window. Before then, the water rushing against the vehicle will make it too hard for you to open a door or window.

If your vehicle is stalled in floodwater, escape as soon as possible.

What if

YOU SEE A DOWNED POWER LINE?

What if you're running to high ground and you see a downed power line? Stay away! Power lines are dangerous in any situation. But they're extra dangerous in a flood. Don't try to walk over them. Don't try to move them. Even if the line isn't sparking, it could be active. If you see someone being shocked by a power line, don't touch the person. The electricity will flow into your body.

There's one exception to the rule of staying away from power lines. If one falls on your car, stay there. If you don't, you'll probably be shocked. Warn anyone who tries to help you to stay far away. Call 911 and wait for rescue workers to arrive.

YOU'RE BEING WASHED AWAY?

You couldn't get to high ground, and now the rushing water is carrying you with it. What do you do now?

All you can do is try to stay afloat. Look for anything that will work as a raft. A piece of wood or a log can be a lifesaver. Grab on and keep your head above the water. Hold on until rescue workers come to help you.

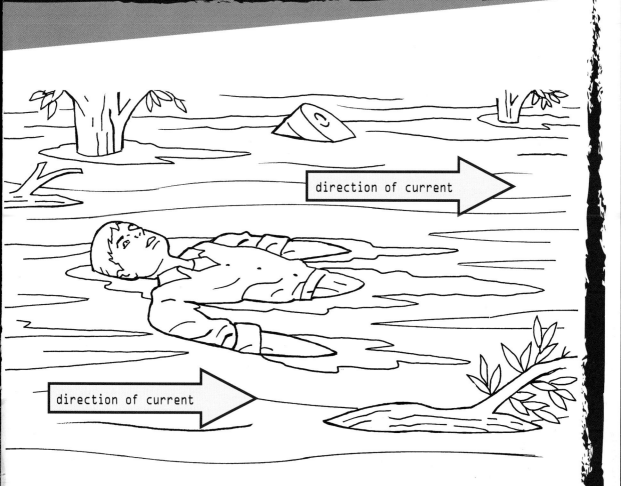

direction of current

direction of current

If you can't find anything to help you float, lie on your back. Point your feet in the direction of the current. Keep looking for tree branches or anything else to grab.

TIP: If you're wearing heavy shoes, kick them off to help you float.

What if

YOU'RE CAUGHT IN A MUDSLIDE?

You may think you're safe if you've reached high ground when the water started to rise. But don't breathe a sigh of relief quite yet. Heavy rains can make soil unstable. If you hear rumbling sounds or loud snapping noises, a mudslide could be headed your way. The rumbling sound could be a huge wall of dirt. The snapping sound may be pipelines or tree branches snapping. Cracks or bulges in the ground are another warning sign. Indoors, you might notice that windows and doors are sticking.

What if you notice a mudslide's warning signs? If you're indoors, go to the highest story. Find the room farthest from the slide. Duck down underneath a sturdy piece of furniture such as a desk or a table.

If you're outside, try to find shelter in a building. If you can't find shelter quickly enough, run downhill at an angle. If the mudslide catches up with you, yell to signal your location to rescue workers. Curl up in a ball and protect your head with your arms.

What if

YOU MEET A SNAKE?

People aren't the only ones driven from their homes by floods. Wild animals may be forced into areas with people. A snake is one critter you won't be happy to see. Most snakes are good swimmers, so they are more likely than other animals to be near you.

Venomous Snakes in North America

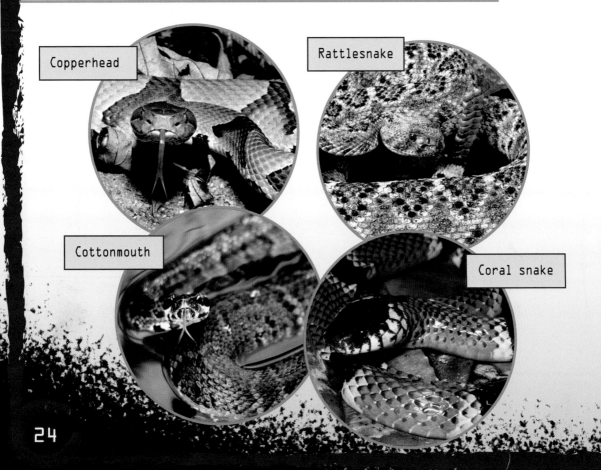

Copperhead

Rattlesnake

Cottonmouth

Coral snake

Venomous snakes are the biggest danger. If you see a rattlesnake, cottonmouth, or another type of venomous snake, keep your distance. Don't make any sudden movements. If you are bitten, take action quickly. If you can, wash the bite. Soap and clean water work best, but even your own saliva can help. Tightly wrap a bandage 2 to 4 inches (5 to 10 centimeters) above the bite. Use your shirt if you don't have anything else. Hold the bitten area below the level of your heart. Get medical attention as soon as you can.

venomous — having or producing a poison called venom

RUNNING FOR HIS LIFE!

Uditha Hettige was eating breakfast near the beach in the country of Sri Lanka on December 26, 2004. Suddenly, he heard birds flying away in a hurry. He looked up and saw a wall of water crashing toward him. While many people stood and watched the wave, Hettige turned and ran for his life.

He sprinted toward higher ground as the wave closed in. He grabbed a young boy who had fallen. He held onto the boy as he climbed a tree. Hettige hung on with all of his strength as the water struck. The force of it tore the boy from his grasp. It even took the wedding ring off his finger. But Hettige held on and survived. More than 100,000 others were killed in the tsunami.

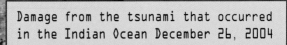

Damage from the tsunami that occurred in the Indian Ocean December 26, 2004

A TSUNAMI HEADS YOUR WAY?

Tsunamis are one of nature's deadliest disasters. Often, they come with little or no warning. But you can watch for clues from nature. Rumbling of the ground in a coastal area is one sign. Birds chirping wildly or other animals suddenly acting strangely are other warning signs.

If the ocean water suddenly draws back, exposing the ocean bottom near the coast, that's a big warning sign. Lots of people walk out to investigate this strange event. That's the worst thing you can do. The water that draws back is going to return in the form of a wave. Run as fast as you can to high ground. Move inland and look for a tall hill or a sturdy structure. Like in any flood, climbing a tree can be a last resort. But tsunamis are especially strong. Even a sturdy tree may not be able to hold up against the force of the water.

When the first wave has passed, stay alert. Most tsunamis include a series of waves. And the first wave isn't always the biggest!

If the water draws back suddenly near the coast, run as fast as you can to higher ground.

SURVIVING THE AFTERMATH

The scariest part of a flood may be long past you. But that doesn't mean the danger is over. Floodwater can weaken walls and ceilings of homes. Severely damaged buildings can collapse. Stay away from buildings that are leaning.

Floodwater also causes many problems inside damaged homes. It often causes mold growth. Breathing in mold spores can make you sick. Floodwater can also spread toxic chemicals. Don't eat food that may have touched the water. Don't drink tap water until local officials tell you the water is safe.

After a flood, be prepared for a long, messy cleanup. If you think cleaning your bedroom is bad, try mopping up backed-up sewage in your basement! In the worst cases, cleaning up after a flood takes years.

Floods are dangerous and destructive. But using basic survival tips will help you stay safe.

spore — a cell produced by fungi or plants; a spore can develop into a new fungus or plant.

MAKE A
SURVIVAL KIT

Prepare for floods and other natural disasters by keeping an emergency survival kit in your home. Put your survival items in a plastic container with a tight lid to keep out water. Keep the kit in a handy place. Everyone in your family should know where the kit is located. Include these items:

1. battery-powered radio
2. flashlight with batteries
3. signal flare
4. first-aid kit
5. 1 gallon (3.8 liters) of bottled water per person, per day
6. three-day supply of canned and other ready-to-eat foods
7. cell phone
8. whistle
9. can opener (non-electric)
10. water purification tablets

11. money (cash) in waterproof container
12. any prescription medications needed for family members
13. extra clothing
14. gas shut-off wrench
15. pet food, if you have pets

Glossary

bacteria (bak-TEER-ee-uh) — one-celled, microscopic living things that exist all around you and inside you; some bacteria cause disease.

current (KUHR-uhnt) — the movement of water

evacuate (i-VA-kyuh-wayt) — to leave an area during a time of danger

flash flood (FLASH FLUHD) — a flood that happens with little or no warning, often during periods of heavy rainfall

hurricane (HUR-uh-kane) — a very large storm with high winds and rain; hurricanes form over warm ocean water.

meteorologist (mee-tee-ur-AWL-uh-jist) — a person who studies and predicts the weather

spore (SPOR) — a cell produced by fungi or plants; a spore can develop into a new fungus or plant.

storm surge (STORM SURJ) — a sudden, strong rush of water that happens as a hurricane moves toward land

toxic (TOK-sik) — poisonous

tsunami (soo-NAH-mee) — a large, destructive wave caused by an underwater earthquake

venomous (VEN-uh-muhss) — having or producing a poison called venom

Read More

Allan, Tony. *Wild Water: Floods.* Turbulent Planet. Chicago: Raintree, 2006.

Currie, Stephen. *Escapes from Natural Disasters.* Great Escapes. San Diego: Lucent Books, 2004.

Fine, Jil. *Floods.* Natural Disasters. New York: Children's Press, 2007.

Internet Sites

FactHound offers a safe, fun way to find educator-approved Internet sites related to this book.

Here's what you do:

1. Visit *www.facthound.com*
2. Choose your grade level.
3. Begin your search.

This book's ID number is 9781429622776.

FactHound will fetch the best sites for you!

Index